Original title:
Between the House and the Sky

Copyright © 2025 Creative Arts Management OÜ
All rights reserved.

Author: Lucas Harrington
ISBN HARDBACK: 978-1-80587-164-4
ISBN PAPERBACK: 978-1-80587-634-2

Heartbeats in the Ether

A squirrel wears a tiny hat,
Dancing on the fence like that,
With acorns flung, he starts to tease,
While birds all laugh and chirp with ease.

The garden gnome has lost his shoe,
He claims it's where the wild things grew,
In tango twirls, they spin around,
While neighbors chuckle at this sound.

The Pull of the Infinite

A kite got caught in Grandma's hair,
She yells with joy, flailing in air,
While dogs all bark at clouds so white,
As kids take off in sheer delight.

The moon comes down to play with stars,
It tickles them, then drives their cars,
As laughter rolls through fields of green,
Where every chuckle's heard and seen.

Flickering Lights Above

The fireflies host a disco night,
With glow sticks dancing, oh, what a sight!
They spin and twirl in pure delight,
While frogs insist they join the flight.

A cat pretends to be a star,
Then jumps too high and falls too far,
With every bounce, a giggle burst,
Cosmic chaos, oh how it thirsts!

Outlines of the Day

The sun flips pancakes, sizzles, and spins,
While shadows play at peek-a-boo wins,
A spoonful of giggles floods the street,
As the crunch of laughter leaves no defeat.

A hedgehog wears a tiny coat,
Riding a turtle on a boat,
With every wave, they splash and grin,
In this funny race, we all win!

Shimmering Veil of Dawn

The rooster's shout wakes up the sun,
Chickens dance, their day begun.
A cat with swagger struts around,
While squirrels plot in leaps and bounds.

Curtains flutter like loyal flags,
The coffee brews, the aroma drags.
A sock escapes, it's on the run,
Chased by laughter, oh what fun!

Notes from the Ether

The postman hums a quirky tune,
As pigeons gossip 'neath the moon.
A mailbox grins, the mail it keeps,
While sleepy dogs embrace their sleeps.

A dragonfly flirts with a bee,
Claiming it's just 'flying free'.
The garden gnome waves a hand,
In a world where silliness is grand.

The Sway of Settled Air

The curtains sway like dancers bold,
While dust motes swirl, their stories told.
A spider spins tales on every thread,
In this circus of life, where we tread.

The ceiling fan plays a game of tag,
As we all giggle, sharing a rag.
The clock ticks loud, but we just sigh,
Time's a joke, we're all that fly!

Reflecting the Essence

Mirrors smile back, with laughter bright,
While toothpaste wars begin the fight.
The floorboards creak a funny song,
Reminding us that nothing's wrong.

In the hallway, photos prance,
A family tree doing a dance.
With echoes of joy, we share a grin,
In this realm, we always win.

Breath of the Evening

As shadows stretch and cats take flight,
The squirrel on the fence plays peek-a-boo at night.
The moon wears a grin, quite cheeky and bold,
While crickets laugh at secrets untold.

The stars in their twinkles exchange silly jokes,
A couple of owls share laughter with folks.
Each breeze seems to giggle, a light-hearted sigh,
As night casts its charm, oh me, oh my!

Dusk's Gentle Embrace

When twilight waltzes with the colors of dusk,
I spot a raccoon, all chubby and brusque.
He's stealing some snacks from the picnic we tossed,
While pesky mosquitoes gainsay, they're lost!

Fireflies gather in a disco of light,
They twirl and they whirl, what a dazzling sight!
With owlish hoots echoing jests through the air,
It seems that the night is good-natured and rare.

Skybound Echoes

Up above, the clouds engage in a race,
While a lone pigeon struts, sporting a grumpy face.
The sun tickles the horizon, a fiery delight,
And birds compete loudly in their morning kite flight.

A balloon floats by, with a 'Hi' and a cheer,
It bobbles and wobbles, it's seeking your ear.
Each whisper of wind seems to giggle and sway,
Making fun of the leaves that just won't obey.

Threshold of Light

At dawn, the world yawns with a big stretch and smile,
While socks rebel, hiding—oh, just for a while!
The sun peeks its head over rooftops and trees,
Tickling the flowers, sending bees to their knees.

With coffee in hand, I sip on a joke,
While the toaster pops bread with a comical poke.
The day's just beginning, oh what a delight,
As giggles and sunshine welcome the light!

In the Embrace of Space

Stars hang like socks on a line,
Aliens snack on our lunch divine.
Planets dance with a wobble and shake,
Comets crash parties for giggles' sake.

Galaxies spin with a wobbly glee,
Asteroids sing in off-key harmony.
Black holes hide while we play peek-a-boo,
Space is our playground, no homework, woohoo!

Twilight's Swaying Heart

The sun hangs low, it's feeling kind,
Kicking clouds with a playful mind.
Twilight giggles, a prankster so sly,
Painting the world in a colorful dye.

Fireflies twirl, a disco in bloom,
Chasing each other in the evening's gloom.
Crickets crack jokes with a chirpy cheer,
Winking at shadows that start to appear.

Window Whispers

Windows creak like they've had too much tea,
Gossiping secrets from you to me.
The curtains dance, twirling in delight,
While dust bunnies chuckle at their flight.

In the nook, a spider spins tales of old,
With eight tiny legs, it's daring and bold.
Each night they weave stories so sly,
While we dream big, beneath the sky.

The Space Where Dreams Converge

In the realm where dreams come to play,
Clouds are pillows for thoughts in dismay.
Doodles of wishes float high and wide,
With laughter as light as a joyful tide.

Kites of ambition soar, twist, and twirl,
As stardust unfurls in a cosmic swirl.
Whimsical wonders tickle the air,
In this land of fun, there's plenty to share.

The Silence of Open Air

In the yard, I lost my shoe,
A gopher claimed it, who knew?
It twirls around like it's a star,
As I laugh at life's bizarre.

The wind whispers silly dreams,
Of squirrels in top hats, it seems.
A breeze tickles my nose just right,
And I giggle at this newfound flight.

Breathing in the Breath of Stars

I tried to breathe in cosmic dust,
But ended up with a sneeze, I must.
The Milky Way laughs, a twinkling delight,
As I dance with comets under moonlight.

Stars winking in a planetary game,
They jest at my clumsy, foolish fame.
I reach for one and spill my tea,
The universe giggles, oh, what glee!

Bridges to the Celestial

Clouds are just marshmallows on high,
I'm a kid again, soaring through the sky.
With sprinkles of humor up in the air,
I build bridges made of silly flair.

A rocket made of laundry, what a sight!
The moon winks at my funny plight.
Stars are just lights on this ragged path,
The cosmos chuckles at my childlike laugh.

The Dance of Light and Shadow

In shadows, I see a disco beat,
As sunbeams bob around my feet.
A dance party with dust bunnies in tow,
We spin and twirl, putting on a show.

The walls creak with laughter, oh what fun,
In this wild ballet under the sun.
I stumble, I giggle, I jump with glee,
With each fall, the shadows dance with me.

Conversations with the Clouds

I asked a cloud what it would wear,
It said, "I'll sport a sunset flare!"
I joked, "How about a dress of rain?"
It laughed and said, "No, that's insane!"

A fluffy friend rolled by my side,
Claiming it could float and glide.
I told it, "Don't go too high up,"
It grinned, "I'll spill my drink in your cup!"

A thunderhead chimed in, quite bold,
"I've seen the world, both young and old."
I winked and said, "Tell me your tales,"
It coughed and thundered, "Wish I had scales!"

In perfect jest, they danced and swirled,
Crashing like a giggling world.
I stood below, just laughing free,
While clouds above cracked jokes with glee.

Shadows at Twilight

As sun dipped low, the shadows crept,
They whispered secrets while I slept.
A gnome complained of not much light,
A squirrel debated, "Who's wrong or right?"

A cat-shaped shadow stretched with grace,
Claiming it could win a race.
I said, "But it's not about the speed,"
"It's all about the mischief, indeed!"

The blooms at dusk began to yawn,
Their petals drooped, feeling so drawn.
A shadow laughed and poked the rest,
"Buds, don't fret, I'm still the best!"

Then with a wink, the moon emerged,
And all the shadows joyfully surged.
They danced in twirls, in funny styles,
As night descended with laughter and smiles.

The Edge of Ordinary

At the brink of the day, all seemed plain,
Till a cat in a hat danced on a train.
"Choo-choo!" it cried, with a flick of its tail,
"While I sip my tea, I'll not derail!"

Along came a dog in mismatched shoes,
Said, "Hey, what's this? I brought some blues!"
The cat replied, "Please, not too loud,
Let's stay quirky, let's feel proud!"

A tree started giggling, swaying with glee,
"It's not every day you meet such a spree!"
"I'll juggle some apples, if that's all right,"
While everyone cheered in the fading light.

Just at the edge of what we know,
Magic springs from the ordinary show.
With quirks and laughs, they painted the scene,
At the brink of the day, of fun and serene.

Dividing Line of Air

A whisper floated on a breeze,
With giggles caught among the trees.
A squirrel claimed it owned the gust,
"Step back, fellas, in trees I trust!"

The birds debated who sung best,
A wren and robin took their test.
The wind just chuckled, holding tight,
"I'll make you all sound out of sight!"

The butterflies caught in playful spin,
Said, "Let's play hide and seek again!"
But just as they flitted here and there,
A gust came by to stir their hair.

So on this line, where giggles meet,
All creatures share a funny feat.
In the airy world, it's light and clear,
Making friends with laughter near.

Whispers of the Atmosphere

Up above, the clouds are near,
A squirrel yelled, 'Hey, come here!'
The birds fly by with such a sigh,
While marshmallows float, oh my, oh my!

Raindrops dance like tiny feet,
Wearing hats, oh what a treat!
A breeze that tickles all around,
Makes me giggle at the sound.

Embracing the Vastness

In the wide blue, kites will glide,
With goofy faces as they ride.
A plane zooms by with a funny honk,
While butterflies play on a leafy bonk!

The sun wears shades, it's far too bright,
The moon can't help but twinkle, right?
A comet swoops, oh what a sight,
We laugh and wave with pure delight.

Moments of Stillness

A cloud sits still, just like a chair,
While ants gather for a fair.
They barter crumbs and take a stand,
Sipping tea from a tiny hand!

The sky waits for the lightning's joke,
While wise old owls start to poke.
'Who's there?' they hoot as thunder cracks,
And giggles echo through the cracks.

The Quiet Above

At twilight, stars begin to hum,
While crickets voice their evening drum.
Clouds whisper secrets, oh so sly,
As shadows dance, and fireflies fly!

The moon is grinning with a cheer,
While night birds croon with no fear.
A soft breeze carries laughs and tales,
In the cozy vault where mischief prevails.

Whispers of the Horizon

The sun gets shy as night draws near,
While cats in hats stir up their cheer.
With owls that giggle and stars that wink,
They tease the moon with a playful wink.

A breeze that chuckles, sways the trees,
While squirrels shout, "We've got the keys!"
To doors of laughter, secrets bright,
In corners cozy, they laugh all night.

Where Shadows Greet the Clouds

Up high the shadows learn to dance,
With clouds that twirl in a feathered trance.
A lizard in glasses joins the fun,
Reciting jokes to the setting sun.

They giggle about the length of grass,
And how swiftly the moments pass.
Through whispered secrets aloft and free,
The sky holds jokes for you and me.

Echoes of Earth and Ether

Where earthworms laugh and raindrops race,
A riddle hides in this merry place.
With every plop on a muddy shoe,
A rhyme escapes for me and you.

The daisies know the latest tea,
While breezes tend to spill with glee.
Echoes bounce from flowers to the moon,
In the harmony of a silly tune.

The Space Where Dreams Take Flight

In realms where pie flies in the mist,
And flying fish can't resist the twist.
The stars all giggle, twinkling bright,
Like toddlers chasing fireflies at night.

A balloon parade floats by with cheer,
As dreams wave hello, drawing near.
In this wacky world where wishes spin,
There's always fun if you just dive in.

Nature's Surreal Canvas

In a land where trees wear hats,
And squirrels dance like cats,
The flowers giggle as they sway,
While clouds plot mischief every day.

With bunnies hopping on blue thrones,
And frogs reciting funny tones,
The birds all sing in silly tunes,
As butterflies play hopscotch with the moons.

Sunlight tickles the fluffy grass,
While shadows chase the giggles passed,
A rainbow slides down a tree trunk,
As nature winks and gives a funk.

So come and join this wild affair,
Where laughter floats in the bright air,
With every step a twist of fun,
In this canvas, joy is never done!

Under the Canopy of Wishes

Beneath a roof of leafy green,
Where mushrooms wear the silliest sheen,
The foxes chuckle at the clouds,
While laughter echoes, loud and proud.

A raccoon wears a tiny tie,
As ants parade, oh my, oh my!
With every wish that's tossed in flight,
The stars giggle, twinkling bright.

Tucked beneath the wobbly trees,
The breeze tells jokes that tease and please,
A shiny acorn claims its fame,
As crickets chirp the punchline's name.

So gather 'round this vibrant space,
Where dreams explode in a cozy race,
Each wish a balloon, full of surprise,
In this canopy, joy never dies!

The Edge of Earthly Dreams

On the cliff where giggles fall,
With sleepy clouds that start to sprawl,
The stones play hopscotch, nice and bold,
While butterflies whisper secrets untold.

Penguins slide down from the stars,
While elephants dance with old guitars,
A kite gets tangled in the trees,
As time slips by with the greatest ease.

The moon hides under a quilt of dew,
As playful shadows continue to brew,
Each star a friend that winks and nods,
In this fun land, we laugh with the gods.

So step right up to this happy edge,
Where dreams are stitched on a vibrant pledge,
With silliness swirling in every beam,
Join the laughter of earthly dreams!

Threads of Sky Interwoven

Up in the threads where blue meets cheer,
A cat in a balloon gives a murmur so clear,
With starlight spinning in playful sways,
Each moment here is a giggle ballet.

Frogs wear hats made of daisy chains,
While owls play chess and forget their brains,
The sun dips low with a wink and a grin,
As nighttime whispers where fun shall begin.

Clouds knit sweaters snug and tight,
For the breezes dancing in the night,
Where wishes giggle in jumbled heaps,
And the moon croons lullabies that leap.

So follow the threads, let laughter flow,
In this tapestry where fancies glow,
The sky's alive with dreams in tow,
As humor and joy together grow!

Wanderlust of the Spirit

A pigeon's dance upon the breeze,
Chasing dreams with clumsy ease.
It struts like royalty in tow,
To find a snack is its true show.

A squirrel plans a grand escape,
With acorn hat and leafy cape.
He leaps from branch to branch with style,
And winks at us with cheeky guile.

The clouds above begin to giggle,
As raindrops start their playful wiggle.
They tease the earth with wet ballet,
While all the umbrellas hide away.

In every corner of the park,
A laughing child ignites a spark.
With ice cream cones all sticky sweet,
They dance on sidewalks with happy feet.

Spaces Where Light Falls

A cat sprawled wide on a sunlit mat,
Dreaming of catching the quickened rat.
It yawns and stretches in lazy grace,
While shadows plot in the same old place.

The sunbeams giggle as they play,
With dust motes swirling in their ray.
They tickle the nose of an unsuspecting friend,
As laughter echoes that seems to transcend.

A butterfly flutters like a curious thought,
Forgettable yet, it dances untaught.
In a cartoonish twirl, off it goes,
Sneaking up on a flower for a quick nose-to-nose.

The world spins 'round in a merry whirl,
Where light spills softly and giggles unfurl.
In those warm pockets of glowing cheer,
Even the grumpiest hearts can't stay austere.

The Touch of Beyond

A kite takes flight, a colorful spree,
It thinks it's a bird, as wild as can be.
With strings that tangle in clueless delight,
It's a combatant ready for a feathered fight.

The skydiver shouts from the plane up high,
"I hope my parachute won't make me cry!"
We laugh as he tumbles, a tumbleweed free,
Promising laughter and not a catastrophe.

In a garden where gnomes hold a conference,
They discuss in whispers, "What's next in defense?"
With hats so pointy, they lose their poise,
As the wind snickers at their tiny ploys.

Even the moon rolls its eyes so bright,
At comets who think they can dance through the night.
With antics galore in the vast open space,
The universe twirls with a chuckle in place.

Celestial Interludes

Stars twinkle like mischievous children,
Dressed in glitter, they frolic and chidden.
They peek through windows of sleepy towns,
Sprinkling wishes that make us frowns.

A meteor zips past with a wink,
"Catch me if you can!" it seems to think.
A playful chase across the night,
With astronauts giggling in pure delight.

The planets orbit in a grand parade,
Where Saturn wears rings that never fade.
Each orb rolls on, with a laugh so grand,
Creating a cosmic, light-hearted band.

Yet comets crash with blush so red,
Leaving trails of giggles in their stead.
Across the dark, sweet jokes are spun,
In the dance of the night, all laughter won.

The Breath of Twilight

As daylight dips in a goofy frown,
The clouds dance up like a jester's gown.
With twilight's breath, the stars jump high,
And trees look dapper in their black tie.

A squirrel juggles acorns with flair,
While fireflies flicker without a care.
The moon winks down with a silly grin,
"Join the fun, let the night begin!"

The owls hoot jokes from their lofty perch,
As crickets sing songs that sometimes lurch.
The breeze chuckles softly, teasing the night,
"Don't trip on dreams, hold on tight!"

With shadows stretching in playful prance,
Every critter joins in the twilight dance.
So let the laughter echo till dawn,
In the world between dusk and the morn!

Spheres of Solitude

In the morning light, a tumbleweed rolls,
Whispering secrets of forgotten souls.
Each blade of grass plays hide and seek,
While the sun giggles, peeking from a creek.

A lone balloon drifts in merry flight,
Chasing away the troublesome night.
"Excuse me, clouds, will you pass the day?"
And the birds tweet back to have their say.

Mice plotting cheese heists under the moon,
Make cheese puns that make the night swoon.
The stars throw a party, all dressed in light,
While shadows hold hands, too shy for flight.

In this silly dance of solitude found,
The laughter of nature is all around.
With each fleeting moment, the jesters cheer,
While solitude wraps us, warm and near!

Between Grass and Stars

A tangle of weeds has a story to tell,
Of a garden party gone bloomin' well.
The daisies boast of their sunny flair,
While the dandelions float in midair.

A grasshopper plays hopscotch, just for fun,
Bouncing in patterns, oh what a run!
The moon giggles at the silly sight,
"Who knew the earth was so full of light?"

Ants march in lines with their tiny feet,
Dancing in rhythm to the night's heartbeat.
"Pass the crumbs!" cries a voice from the ground,
As the fireflies twinkle all around.

The stars above and the grass below,
Share chuckles and whispers in twilight's glow.
In the cosmic play, no detail's too small,
And laughter erupts like a thunderous call!

The Transition of Time

Tick-tock goes the clock with a cheeky jest,
Frolicking moments, a playful quest.
"Time's a juggler!" says the sun with glee,
"Catch me if you can," he shouts in spree.

Hours twist like pretzels, whirling around,
In the dizzy daze, no logic is found.
A cat naps on minutes, purring its song,
Dreaming of fish that don't take long.

Pigeon coos loudly, a stand-up routine,
Cracking up clouds with jokes in between.
"Who stole my hour?!" the sadness of noon,
Echoes in twilight as fireflies swoon.

Night sways in rhythm, a dance of delight,
With moonbeams glimmering, holding on tight.
The transition of time, a whimsical play,
Where each tick and tock sparks laughter's array!

Fragments of Evening Air

The cat's on the roof, quite high,
Gazing down with a discerning eye.
A bird flies by, doing a twist,
The cat thinks, "Oh, I would insist!"

The sun dips low, painting the ground,
With colors too silly to be found.
A light breeze snickers, a gentle tease,
As leaves shake hands with tiny bees.

Neighbors shout, a mix of cheer,
To call their kids, they're quite sincere.
But the kids run off, playing at large,
While the dog thinks he's set to charge.

In this hour of laughter and play,
The world feels strange in the best way.
With silly stories light as air,
Fragments of joy, drifting everywhere.

Conversations with the Wind

The wind whispers secrets, quite absurd,
Tickling the trees, causing a stir.
"Hey, look over here!" it slyly boasts,
As kites tumble down like playful ghosts.

Squirrels stop to listen, ears on high,
Taking notes, as if to reply.
Their little tails twitch in sheer delight,
At what the wind claims is pure insight.

Clouds roll by, wearing silly hats,
Declaring themselves the kings of chats.
They laugh and puff, in a soft ballet,
As birds join in, singing jokes all day.

In this strange chat with nature's glee,
Each gust and breeze sets the heart free.
Funny exchanges that make life bright,
As the sun winks, bidding goodnight.

Upon the Threshold of Blue

At dusk we step, oh, what a sight,
The world takes on a glow, so light.
A dog barks loud, catching a star,
While kids on bikes ride near and far.

A cat, a hat, and a winsome cow,
All stand in line, not knowing how.
They gossip and giggle, with much delight,
Who'd think such odd friends could unite?

Jellybeans rain from the fading sun,
While laughter bounces, pure fun.
A rabbit hops in, joining the dance,
With a wobbly wiggle, taking a chance.

Forever in wonder, this quirky show,
Makes hearts giggle and spirits glow.
Upon the threshold, every sight,
Transforms the evening into pure light.

The Realm of Endless Possibilities

In a meadow of dreams, where daisies play,
A frog in a top hat shouts, "Hip-hip-hooray!"
He dances with flowers, twirling with glee,
While butterflies giggle, as silly as can be.

A snail with a backpack slides down a path,
Planning an adventure, engaging in math.
He calculates routes to the nearest tightrope,
Dreaming of high-flying, beyond what we hope.

Clouds lose their shape, making a blend,
Of creatures and castles that twist and intend.
An octopus juggles odd shapes in the air,
Drawing smiles from all who stop and stare.

In this realm, where rules take a break,
Fun and laughter are all that's at stake.
Endless possibilities linger and tease,
As reality giggles, caught in the breeze.

Beneath the Eaves of Infinity

A cat on a roof thinks it's grand,
It watches the world, a regal stand.
With squirrels as subjects, it plots a heist,
Dreaming of fish, oh what a feast!

The clouds roll by, like cotton candy,
The dog below thinks it's all just dandy.
"Why chase a tail," the cat would say,
"When I can nap till the end of the day?"

Rain drops like marbles from way up high,
Each one a splash makes the cat sigh.
"Not another shower, oh what a bore,"
As it dreams of lounging on sunshine galore.

The moon peeks in with a mischievous grin,
Waving at cats with a cheeky spin.
Under this roof where the funny things lay,
Life's a wild circus, come join the play!

Skylines and Secrets Unveiled

The city bounds with towers of dreams,
Every window a secret, or so it seems.
They whisper to rooftops and giggle in breeze,
Where pigeons are spies, no doubt they tease.

A bird is perched, plotting its flight,
"Why swoop like an eagle when I'm small and slight?"
Yet it dives for crumbs with such snazzy flair,
Who knew that a city could offer such fare?

Traffic below honks in playful duet,
While cyclists zoom, causing mild regret.
The lights twinkle bright, a mischievous wink,
"Do cars make a wish each time they clink?"

As stars laugh along with the buzzing ground,
Stories are traded without making a sound.
In this great expanse, absurdity thrives,
Where each day is a journey, hilarious lives!

A Tapestry of Dusk and Dawn

At dawn, the toaster pops with a cheer,
"Start your day right, now gather near!"
With buttered toast and tea on the side,
Life's morning giggles, nothing to hide.

The sunset wears a flamboyant dress,
Each hue a laugh, nature's finesse.
As birds perform their aerial ballet,
They jest with the wind, come join the fray!

Stars twinkle out like fairy lights,
Sprinkling wishes on whimsical flights.
"Why walk when you can dance on the way?"
The moon chimes in, in a silvery sway.

In this vast opus, the day plays its part,
Layered with giggles, stitching the heart.
Each moment a thread, spun with delight,
Crafting a canvas where laughter takes flight!

Streets That Kiss the Heavens

The pavement dreams of floating high,
With every crack, a secret sigh.
"Just one step more to tickle the clouds!"
It whispers to shoes, "Come join the crowds!"

Beneath the lampposts, shadows dance free,
Each flicker a giggle, oh can't you see?
A bicycle zooms, almost takes flight,
Riding the wind, what a silly sight!

The benches all chuckle, sharing some tea,
"Did you hear about that old maple tree?"
It dropped its leaves in a flamboyant swirl,
While kids laugh and chase, giving it twirl.

The sky's a performer, and we all play along,
Joining this rhythm, we hum a sweet song.
In these joking streets, we all find a way,
To turn the mundane into a dance every day!

Fragments of Serenity

Clouds parade like busy bees,
Tickling roofs with gentle tease.
A cat's on the sill, dreaming wide,
Chasing shadows, a playful ride.

Windows open, ears exposed,
Laughing at the neighbor's woes.
The squirrels stack acorns high,
As birds argue their latest lie.

Pigeons coo in perfect tune,
While kids play pitched games at noon.
A breeze whispers jokes untold,
In the sun, where warmth unfolds.

Skyward Gazes

I saw a cloud pretend to fly,
With wings made of cotton, oh my!
A dog thinks it's royalty,
Sniffing grass like it's a decree.

Kites tango with the gentle wind,
Laughter loops—a playful spin.
A toddler shouts, "Look, it's free!"
While ducks embrace the air with glee.

The sun winks large, a golden fool,
Dancing near the old school pool.
I chuckle at shadows that tease,
As life rolls brisk, like autumn leaves.

Sounds of a Fading Sun

The sun burps softly, day's last sip,
As crickets start their nightly trip.
A distant laugh rolls through the air,
While twilight teases without a care.

Fireflies wink like rowdy stars,
Guiding home the light of jars.
A saxophone plays notes of fun,
With squirrels grooving, one by one.

A bat swoops down for another round,
While toads croak like a grumpy sound.
Late-night snacks, oh such a treat,
As shadows dance on gusty street.

The Allure of Open Space

Fields stretch wide, like dreams unbound,
Where laughter is the only found.
A pickle jar spills on the grass,
As ants line up, a feast to amass.

The breeze tells secrets to the trees,
While ticklish blades tease our knees.
A kite in despair, tangled in thorns,
Laughs at the field's gentle scorns.

Hats fly high on the headless bold,
As soft chaos begins to unfold.
Chasing bubbles, we lose track of time,
In this wild place, happiness climbs.

The Cornerstone of Wonder

The mailbox dances with a grin,
It waits for letters that never win.
The garden gnomes play chess at night,
With little hats and eyes so bright.

The cat wears shades, a stylish brat,
He sits and judges every chat.
The wind whispers jokes through the trees,
While squirrels mimic karate with ease.

The lawnmower grows tired of its race,
Complains about this endless space.
The swings creak tales of distant lands,
While stick figures perform magic handstands.

A broom's on strike, trapped in a spot,
Refusing to sweep because it's hot.
The porch light flickers like a disco ball,
As shadows dance and take the fall.

Between the Leaves and the Stars

A squirrel in boots struts by the tree,
Claiming it's the 'squirreliest' of spree.
The moon plays peekaboo with the sun,
Laughing as day and night run.

A ladybug starts a fashion show,
While fireflies argue on who'll glow.
The branches swing like they're on a ride,
With whispers of giggles that won't subside.

The stars hold hands, skip through the night,
In twinkling shoes, flashing bright.
Clouds laugh out loud with popcorn in tow,
Making shadows on the ground below.

A breeze waltzes with the petals below,
Their giggly whispers, a melody slow.
While owls hoot jokes they can't quite recall,
As laughter echoes, a whimsical call.

Chasing Daylight

The sun's a golden pizza slice,
Chasing shadows, oh, isn't that nice?
Clouds are napping in cottony plots,
While daisies argue on sunspot spots.

A rabbit hops with a clock in paw,
Saying, 'I'm late!' with a comical draw.
Butterflies twirl in a dazzling ballet,
As time seems to giggle and play.

Chasing the dawn, a rooster's outdone,
He missed his alarm, now isn't that fun?
The grasshoppers host a morning rave,
Jumping to beats they're all brave.

With yawning trees stretching up high,
Sharing secrets on how to fly.
Daylight laughs, a split-second tease,
As night's shadows dance, oh what a breeze!

The Space Beyond the Threshold

The door creaks open with a sigh,
Whispers secrets from days gone by.
A rug rolls up, ready to flee,
While the cat stares as if it sees.

The hallway twists like a curly fry,
Painting the walls with dreams awry.
A pair of shoes debates their fate,
Should they wait, or should they skate?

The coat rack blushes, embarrassed too,
With memories of parties, a lively crew.
And lights blink on like they can't believe,
That life's a joke we all perceive.

Mirrors giggle at their own reflections,
Creating quirky, wild connections.
While a vacuum grumbles, 'Not my shift!'
As dust bunnies plot, making their drift.

Beneath the Open Horizon

A squirrel wore a tiny hat,
Chasing shadows with a spat.
The breeze laughed and swayed the trees,
As birds chirped jokes, feeling at ease.

Butterflies raced the wind's soft sigh,
While ants debated the best pie.
A ladybug twirled with a grin,
In a dance where all could win.

The clouds giggled, fluffy and round,
As daisies laughed from the ground.
A rabbit jumped, tripped on a shoe,
Said, 'This is not what bunnies do!'

Meanwhile, the sun winked, glowing bright,
Casting shadows that danced with delight.
Every corner held a tale,
In this realm where laughter set sail.

The Dance of Day and Night

The moon wore shades, strutting with flair,
While the sun tried to fix its hair.
Stars in the night whispered sweet tunes,
To crickets playing quirky bassoons.

Dusk rolled in with a twirl and a spin,
As daylight blushed and tried to fit in.
The owls chimed in with clever quips,
While shadows practiced their dance flips.

A comet swooped with a chuckle and grin,
And said, 'Come join, let's all spin!'
They twirled through the sky, a dizzying sight,
As laughter echoed deep in the night.

Just as the stars began to snore,
The sun peeked in, saying, 'One more!'
And so the cycle danced like no other,
In a world where time couldn't bother.

Sunlit Pathways

A pathway danced in sunlit glee,
With flowers making quite the spree.
A beetle wore a tiny red coat,
While bugs on the fence crafted a moat.

Each pebble sang a quirky tune,
As the breeze brought in a fluffy balloon.
Children raced with giggles galore,
Chasing shadows that begged for more.

A tree offered shade, winking on cue,
While squirrels juggled acorns for you.
The sun shot rays like playful darts,
While birds performed on their tiny parts.

Every step was a hop, skip, and laugh,
On pathways where time took a bath.
As dusk approached with a soft, warm sigh,
Nature chuckled, 'Oh, my, oh my!'

Where Ground Meets Infinity

A worm in a top hat wrote a script,
For a play where the clouds would flip.
Grass blades cheered, ready to perform,
As daisies twirled in floral swarm.

The horizon stretched, tired of the show,
Said, 'Why not join? Let's make it glow!'
With laughter, the ground met the stars,
In a cosmic party without any bars.

The wind became the favorite bard,
As it told tales that left them charred.
An ant slipped backstage, took a bow,
While the sun cheered, 'Look at us now!'

And so in this realm of whimsical might,
Where laughter erupted day and night,
Every creature joined in the fun,
In a dance with no end, just begun.

Footsteps on Cloud Dances

Up on fluffy clouds, they bounce around,
Sneaky little footsteps make a silly sound.
The sunbeam whispers jokes so bright,
While giggling stars join the playful flight.

A feathered friend with a wobbly beak,
Tells funny tales that make us squeak.
We dance with grace, yet trip and fall,
Laughing so hard, we're having a ball.

With every leap, a puff of fluff,
Turns into giggles; oh, it's just enough!
Catch those moments, don't let them fly,
For who could resist a fun cloud high?

As laughter mingles with cotton candy,
The sky might seem a little dandy.
So let's prance up high, with joy in our feet,
In this fluffy playground, life is sweet!

The Twilight Interval

At dusk where sun and stars collide,
A coyote hums, and a squirrel glides.
The moon peeks out with a cheeky grin,
While answering dreams that dare to begin.

"I'm off to catch a comet," says the owl,
"Just don't tell the rabbits; they might howl!"
A firefly flickers, then starts a bop,
Saying, "Come dance; let's never stop!"

Shadows play tag with the light, so bold,
And crickets cheer, their stories told.
In this twilight interval, joy abounds,
With mischievous creatures and silly sounds.

So let's twirl and swirl beneath the sky,
Where every giggle matters, oh my!
Embrace the sparkle, let your heart race,
In the funny twilight, find your space!

Flora and Firmament

Daisies chat with stars at night,
While lilies laugh in pure delight.
"Hey, did you hear? The tulips sing!
I think the daisies are pranking spring!"

Beneath the moon, the poppies sway,
Telling secrets of the day.
"Oh, come now, let's play hide and seek,
But watch out for critters; they're quite unique!"

With petals bright and giggles loud,
The flora forms a silly crowd.
The firmament grins, a trusty friend,
As laughter flows; it'll never end.

So dance along this flowery trail,
Painted with laughter, stories prevail.
In this garden of joy, we'll always find,
Nature's humor is one of a kind!

Pathways of Possibility

Here's a path made of marshmallow dreams,
Where laughter flows like bubbling streams.
A squirrel in shades struts with pride,
As butterflies cheer from the other side.

"Take a left at the giggling tree,
Or right past the flower that dances with glee!"
What a ride, everyone's in the game,
Each twist and turn is wild and untame!

Jellybean rocks clutter the trail,
With every step, there's a story to hail.
So map your course through the humorous twist,
And don't be surprised if you bump into mist!

On these pathways where smiles arise,
With every detour, a new surprise.
Take a leap, prance, or simply skip,
In these pathways of fun, let life rip!

Nestled in Between

A cat in a hat, oh what a sight,
Chasing its tail in the morning light.
A squirrel with style, dancing on air,
With acorns for shoes, it's quite a affair.

A dog doing yoga, twists like a pretzel,
While birds in the trees are finding their mettle.
An ant on a skateboard, slicker than ice,
Claims all of the crumbs, oh, isn't that nice?

A frog in a tux, jumps with such flair,
While butterflies giggle, floating up there.
The grass plays a tune, it's a croaky ballet,
In this whimsical spot, we could laugh all day.

So join the parade, let the laughter begin,
With froggy maestro leading the din.
In this cozy nook, under sunbeam's sheen,
All creatures unite, in this fun-filled scene.

Where the Ground Meets the Glitter

A bear in a bowtie, struts down the lane,
Dreams of a picnic, with jam on his brain.
The ground's made of cookies, oh what a treat,
Teddy bears chuckle, while they munch on sweet.

A rabbit in shades, lounging with style,
Winks at the clouds, in a casual smile.
While grasshoppers tap dance, on delicate toes,
And ladybugs cheer, in their polka-dot clothes.

The sun-flowers gossip, revealing their secrets,
While ducks in a row debate the best regrets.
With whispers of cookies, and plans for a show,
The ground and the glitter have nowhere to go.

So if you stop by where silliness spreads,
Join the wild party, leave worry in shreds.
Laugh with the critters, enjoy every bit,
In this sparkly place, where giggles are lit.

Ascendance of the Ordinary

An old shoe can dance without missing a beat,
Twirling on sidewalks while tapping its feet.
A mailbox is buzzing with gossip so fine,
While the postman performs a most curious line.

A lamp with a smile, shines bright in the night,
Winks at the stars, a most comical sight.
The fence sings a tune about love and retreat,
While hedgehogs debate if the thorns are too sweet.

A pancake rises, adorned with a hat,
Confidently flips, with a squishy spat.
Meanwhile, a garden hose tells tales of old,
Of summer adventures, both funny and bold.

In this odd little realm, where the normal can prance,
Everyday objects take part in the dance.
With laughter and joy, in a splendid array,
The ordinary shines in a humorous way.

The Gap of Wonder

A snail in a race with a mouse and a bee,
Stretches out slow, says, "Just wait for me!"
The clouds all chuckle, oh what a delight,
As flowers bloom giggling under morning light.

A kite seeks the ground, gets tangled in twigs,
While fish in the pond throw a party for pigs.
A turtle with glasses reads stories aloud,
To a gathering curious and ever so proud.

The sun dons a wig and twirls in a spin,
While chickens in hats join in for the win.
The bees wear bow ties, and the worms dance a jig,
In this charming place, even grasshoppers dig.

So wander along where the whimsy is found,
In this gap filled with wonder, where joy knows no bound.

With laughter aplenty, and silly delight,
The magic of moments can sparkle so bright.

Sketches in the Breeze

A squirrel in a tutu spins,
While wind collects his nuts and wins.
A cat chases clouds with glee,
As laughter bounces from tree to tree.

The ducks debate in hats so tall,
Who'll be the next to take a fall?
A frog hops in with shiny pants,
And all the trees begin to dance.

Breezes giggle, tickle the grass,
As turtles waddle, slow but brash.
The sun winks down, with rays so bright,
And everything feels just right.

Creativity's a wild, mad chase,
Where even the wind finds its place.
Sketches flutter on unseen hands,
As mischief unfolds in nature's bands.

The Meeting of Elements

Water met fire for a chat,
'You're too hot,' said water, 'what's up with that?'
Earth rolled in with a playful grin,
'You're both so silly, let's all just spin!'

Air chimed in, 'Let's lighten the mood,
I'll whirl around like a funky dude!'
Together they giggled, tossed ideas wide,
As clouds rolled in for a joyride.

Earth spilled some rocks just for fun,
While fire sent sparks, 'Look, I can run!'
Water splashed back, 'That tickles my toes!'
And laughter echoed where the wild wind blows.

Amidst this chaos, they took a breath,
Not quite a party, more a banquet of jest.
With elements mingling, chaos reigned high,
As stars winked down from the vast clear sky.

A Horizon Untamed

Look at that line where the sun does peek,
Where shadows ignore the truth we seek.
The horizon dances, oh what a sight,
With colors that giggle and tease the night.

Clouds argue on who can look more grand,
While birds play tag, making their stand.
The grass rolls laughter, yellow and green,
As ants march by with a frenzy of sheen.

There's a rabbit with dreams of flying so high,
Saying, 'One day I'll give it a try!'
While crickets strum a tune quite absurd,
And every note is a joyous word.

At the edge of the world, where silly things grow,
All creatures giggle, putting on a show.
In the wild, untamed twilight's embrace,
Life's a circus, a riotous space.

Echoes of Nightfall

As daylight fades into a wink,
The stars gather round for a drink.
'Cheers!' they shout in twinkling glee,
As shadows stretch, 'Can you see me?'

The moon dons a cap, oh what a sight,
Swears he's ready to rule the night.
Bats crack jokes about the sun's retreat,
While owls compete in the wisdom seat.

Whispers of crickets hum through the dark,
Each note a giggle, a twinkling spark.
Frogs croak verses of wild delight,
As the world chuckles in soft twilight.

With echoes bouncing, the night comes alive,
Where humor and giggles suddenly thrive.
In this realm of dusk, a playful spree,
Every shadow is just trying to be free.

Tips of Leaves and Clouds

Here's a leaf with a tiny grin,
It thinks it can dance on the wind.
With each gust, it spins and flies,
Waving hello to the silly skies.

A cloud bursts out laughing in white,
Trading its fluff for a kite in flight.
Leaves shout, 'Look! We're astronauts now!
On adventures, we'll learn just how!'

Squirrels giggle high up in trees,
They sneak up to tease the buzzing bees.
'What a plot!' they squeak without care,
'We're launching a squirrel and leaf air fair!'

So up they go, a parade of cheer,
Collecting the good times, spreading the sheer.
The sky takes a bow to the leafy crew,
As laughter echoes, sweet and true.

Traces of Forgotten Dreams

In the corner I found a lost kite,
Dreams tangled up, what a sight!
'Let's fly away!' it squealed in glee,
'Forget the ground, just come with me!'

Old pillows filled with wishes untold,
Cushions grinning like friends of old.
A dream once big, now a fluffy joke,
Laying low, just puffing some smoke.

Tooth fairies whisper, 'We won't forget!
The teeth and the dreams, they're part of the set.'
Clowns come marching, with noses so red,
Traces of laughter bouncing instead.

The night sky yawns, stars take flight,
Together we'll chase the dreams of the night.
With giggles and wiggles, we dance like fools,
In the realm of forgotten magic schools.

Flight Plans of the Soul

A paper plane with a compass so bright,
Asks the sun, 'Where to? Day or night?'
Does it soar to the moon, or a height so grand?
Or seek out mischief in a shadowy land?

Happy horizons are asking for fun,
With ticklish breezes, they're on the run.
Clouds in their ways, spinning tales of old,
While little birds jest about being bold.

'Hey you!' squawks a cardinal, flapping near,
'With those flight plans, you're the pilot, dear!'
But the paper plane just giggles and spins,
Ready for adventures where laughter begins.

In the maze of the heavens, joy loves to dwell,
No worries, no hurries, just a whimsical spell.
The soul in the airwaves, carefree and whole,
Glides on giggles, it's a flight of the soul.

The Path of a Wayward Wind

Oh, the wind went straying, what a roam,
Curly-twirly, it thought it was home.
Jumping over fences, whispering low,
Searching for laughter, where do winds go?

Bouncing off rooftops, dancing through eaves,
Tickling the branches of whimsical leaves.
A snail looked up and said with a wink,
'Chase your own tail, you'll know what I think!'

With a whoosh and a rush, the wind slipped away,
Ffancying tea with a cloud for the day.
They chuckle and sip, oh, what a delight,
In the warmth of the stars that blanket the night.

As shadows grow long, and giggles entwine,
The breeze winks to the moon, says, 'You're divine!'
So come, take a trip on this whimsical ride,
For the path of the wind is a joyous glide.

Ribbons of Existence

Up high I see the birds go past,
Wearing tiny hats, so oddly fast.
Their chatter tickles the clouds above,
While squirrels dance in a velvet glove.

The sun plays peekaboo with the moon,
As cows try to sing a silly tune.
A kite gets stuck in a tree so tall,
It shouts for help, but no one's on call.

Rainbows wear pajamas, striped and bright,
Sneaking through gardens in the soft twilight.
Pumpkins roll laughing down the lane,
Singing praises to the gentle rain.

Caught in a web of giggles and glee,
Life spins around like a bumblebee.
With every step, I trip on a shoe,
In this odd dance, I'm laughing too!

The Horizon's Secret

The horizon winks, it's quite the tease,
Juggling clouds with effortless ease.
I toss my hat, hoping it'll soar,
But it flops down, like a sleepy boar.

Sunflowers gossip, heads held high,
They're plotting a scheme to tickle the sky.
Meanwhile, ants march in a straight line,
Debating the merits of mustard and vine.

A good-natured breeze flips my pages,
Whispering secrets of wise old sages.
But they're just jokes about squirrels in hats,
Doing the tango with sleeping cats!

The horizon giggles, oh what a show,
Crafting comedy acts in the late afternoon glow.
I laugh along, my heart feeling light,
In this circus of life, every day's a delight!

Embracing the Limitless

Trees wear spectacles, peering around,
They ponder the wonder of the ground.
While turtles play checkers with wispy grass,
Betting their shells on who'll win the class.

A cloud in a scarf spins tales of cheer,
Of adventures taken without any fear.
They say the wind often tells a joke,
It makes the tall grass giggle and poke.

Invisible whispers of laughter float,
As dandelions sail on a tiny boat.
Fish in the pond roll their eyes with glee,
At frogs dressed as kings with crowns made of sea!

Embracing the silly, the grand, and the small,
Life is a carnival, a glittering ball.
A dance with the clouds, a jest with a star,
Who knew the limitless would take us so far?

The Quietude of High Altitudes

Above the mountains, a penguin makes claims,
That he's the best at playing charades.
Cacti are laughing, holding their sides,
As they witness this penguin's wild rides.

The echoes bounce back, a sardonic cheer,
With each silly prank, higher I steer.
A flight of fancy, on a gnarled tree limb,
I wave at a llama, who's trying to swim.

Stars wear pajamas, yawning so wide,
As they watch the mischief down below abide.
Every giggle from up here feels sweet,
Like candy foam rubber on my dancing feet.

In quiet altitudes, where laughter takes flight,
Joy swirls around like a firefly's light.
With all the comedies, life's jesters confer,
In the stillness of peaks, adventures occur!

Celestial Crossover

I saw a cow dance on a star,
As it leaped high, it yelled, "I'm a czar!"
With moonlight boots and a comical glance,
It spun in circles, ready to prance.

A chicken chuckled on a comet's tail,
Singing, "Don't worry, I'll never fail!"
With every flap, it soared with glee,
In a cosmic barnyard, wild and free.

A dog in shades floated by in style,
Holding a drink, it flashed a grin and a smile.
"I'm the king of clouds, don't you see?"
While chasing a squirrel, quite happily.

And a cat on the roof, with a cheeky air,
Claimed, "I own these stars, so you best beware!"
As laughter echoed through the vast expanse,
The universe watched this glitzy dance.

Whispering Winds

The breeze brought tales from who knows where,
Tickling my hair, it made me stare.
"What's this?" I asked, twirling around,
It whispered secrets that spun without sound.

A butterfly busted in with flair,
Saying, "I've wandered beyond, full of air!"
But tripped on a flower, went tumbling down,
And laughed, as it blushed in a fluttery frown.

Leaves chimed in with a rustling cheer,
Singing, "We float with you, lend us your ear!"
They rallied the clouds for a whimsy parade,
While daring the sun to join the charade.

In the midst of giggles, I danced in delight,
With invisible partners, in twilight's light.
The winds may be whispering just like a prank,
But in their cool jest, there's joy to thank.

The Stretch of the Infinite

I reached for the endless, a joyous quest,
And bumped into clouds wearing little vests.
They laughed so loud, turned me upside-down,
"You're doing it wrong, you silly clown!"

One cloud claimed, "I float here all day,
While galaxies spin and comets play.
But watch your step, you might just find,
A wormhole's a-dance, be very kind!"

I tried to walk straight—oh, what a sight!
Tripped on a star, and my shoes took flight.
"Catch those shoes, they've a mind of their own!"
In laughter erupted, I felt so severely prone.

At last, I embraced the cosmic spree,
Floating with planets, oh joyfully free!
In the stretch of the infinite, what a delight,
Where everything's funny and nothing's quite right.

Veils of Azure

Veils of blue danced in the sky,
Winking at me with a playful sigh.
"What's the big deal?" I yelled with glee,
As they tickled my nose, oh, just let me be!

Dancing with shapes that look like cheese,
They floated about, as if to tease.
"You got some imagination, my friend,"
They whispered low, "Come dance till the end!"

A rainbow sneezed, who knew it could?
Floofing about, as only it would.
And every drop of rain that fell,
Brought giggles anew, as I broke my spell.

In veils of azure, laughter took flight,
With colors and dreams, all bold and bright.
The day's gentle pranks made joy resound,
As I twirled and turned on laughter's ground.

www.ingramcontent.com/pod-product-compliance
Lightning Source LLC
Chambersburg PA
CBHW062110280426
43661CB00086B/440